T0228573

BOTTOM

Willy Hudson

BOTTOM

OBERON BOOKS
LONDON
WWW.OBERONBOOKS.COM

First published in 2019 by Oberon Books Ltd
521 Caledonian Road, London N7 9RH
Tel: +44 (0) 20 7607 3637 / Fax: +44 (0) 20 7607 3629
e-mail: info@oberonbooks.com
www.oberonbooks.com

PB ISBN: 9781786827388
E ISBN: 9781786827395

Cover photography by Joe Magowan
Cover design by Jimmy Ginn

10 9 8 7 6 5 4 3 2 1

For Paris

Foreword

My name is Willy Hudson. I moved to London about five years ago. I naïvely moved to chase a guy, but after about two weeks he stopped picking up his phone. I was left feeling pretty lonely, and a bit silly. I didn't know what the fuck I was doing. I didn't want to go back home yet, and I was kind of interested in acting, but had no idea how to make that happen. So, I stuck loads of drugs up my nose and went out all weekend. I worked four zero-hour contract jobs to pay the rent and afford the lifestyle. I quickly got sucked into a hedonistic, distractive and destructive cycle.

I was a Bottom. In every sense. My sex life was shite – I used to think that it didn't matter if I was enjoying it or not, I would just close my eyes and it would be over soon. I only ever had sex when I was smashed, which meant I could hardly get an erection and barely remember what happened. I was reckless with myself and had little self-respect.

I messaged a guy on Tinder. He responded after ONE WHOLE YEAR, but he looked cute and he seemed cool, so I agreed to meet up. The date was fucking glorious. We got some beers and walked around the Olympic Park in Stratford. He told me he had met Beyoncé and I freaked out. We sneaked into the Olympic swimming pool and stood near the edge of the pool in the middle of the night, daring each other to jump in. Both of us trying to impress the other with how far we'd go. Of course, I got scared the security guard would catch us and ran out. I will always kick myself for not having the confidence to let go and jump. It could have been an amazing first date moment, splashing around and being crazy. (And maybe getting arrested.)

A few dates later we tried to have sex. I felt like I needed to be a Top. We hadn't communicated about it, I'd just got this 'vibe' and convinced myself that was what needed to happen. I didn't tell him I'd never done that before. I was sober and so very nervous. I couldn't get an erection, nothing worked, and it was all a big embarrassing mess. I still couldn't jump in the pool, as it were. I didn't talk about it with him and laughed it off.

At the same time as all this, I was taken by a friend to see Bryony Kimmings' show *Fake It 'Til You Make It*. I was broken by that piece, the first time I had cried hard in a theatre. I'd never seen anything like it. I followed Kimmings online and signed up to her workshop on making solo performance. I thought it would be sick if I could make something like *Fake It*.

In the workshop, I made an impulsive decision to explore the Top/Bottom labels as my focus for the week. As we shared our topics to the group some bellend laughed and dismissed my idea, which initially shook me. But everyone else was hugely supportive, and it felt right, so I stuck with it. *Bottom,* in its most fragile form, was slowly hatching.

I began to pick apart the Top/Bottom dynamic and understand its roots. I got lost in queer sexual politics and all these labels within the community. I had always felt I distanced myself from what I saw as 'gay culture' and didn't have many queer friends. I had a lot of internalised homophobia that would take me a while to work through.

As I zoomed out and documented my experience, I could see how my sexual anxiety was not only tied to the fears of being a Top, but also rooted in relationships and my general self-esteem. Having to live and work in London was putting huge pressure on me, and I was barely holding it together. My lifestyle needed to change if I was going to make anything happen and get out of the hole I was in.

The show developed and the swimming pool guy stuck around. I eventually sat him down and finally took one of my first little jumps. I said I'd never been a Top, I had a problem with intimacy and that I was so fucking nervous. He gave me complete support and said he didn't actually mind which position we had sex in. Nearly four years later, I can still get anxious and lose my erections a bit, but I'm learning to be way more vulnerable and honest with him.

Writing and processing *Bottom* has been the most life-changing thing that has ever happened to me ever, ever. It has given me confidence and understanding more than I could have imagined. I owe huge thanks to everyone that has helped along its journey. I am so proud of what we have made. This one is for all the fabulous queers. I hope it entertains, connects and helps.

Willy Hudson

HUGE LOVE & THANX TO

The Arts Council, Soho Theatre, Exeter Phoenix,
The Bike Shed Theatre, Bristol Old Vic Ferment,
Strike A Light, Summerhall, Paines Plough,
The CLF Art Café, The Bunker, Nicholas Hytner,
Ian McKellen, Cameron Mackintosh, Jim Broadbent,
Timothy Sheader, William Village, Iorwerth Mort,
Alec Drysdale, Georgia Robinson, Lilly Burton,
Rachel Quinney, Emily Souter Johnson, Ben Romain,
Jim Goddard, Michelle Barnette, Catherine and
Harry Lemon, Steve and Val Hudson, and my family.
Everyone that has generously supported, donated,
bought tickets, tweeted, and helped make
Bottom happen.

Bottom first opened at Summerhall at the Edinburgh Festival Fringe 2018. It transferred later that year to Soho Theatre, followed by a UK tour.

Writer and Performer	Willy Hudson
Director	Rachel Lemon
Dramaturg	Bryony Kimmings
Lighting Designer	Lucy Adams
Sound Designer	Tic Ashfield
Associate Artist	Paris Augustine
Movement Director	Jess Tucker Boyd
Voice Support	Jake Hassam
Graphic Designer	Jimmy Ginn
Photographer	Joe Magowan
Videographer	Tristan Bell
Marketing & PR	Storytelling PR
Producer	Willy Hudson
	Rachel Lemon
Line Producer	Sofia Stephanou

Supported by The Arts Council, Bristol Old Vic Ferment, Strike A Light, Exeter Phoenix and The Bike Shed Theatre.

Characters

WILLY

LUCY

Notes

There are a number of different performance registers, or 'worlds' – Present Day, Date, Backstory, Restaurant and Sex Facts.

There is space for audience interaction, improvisation and moments for ad-libbing.

BEYONCÉ and **TOPS** are voice recordings, taken from interview clips found on YouTube.

Scene 1

Present Day.

Ideally the stage is in traverse, although the show can be adapted for alternative configurations. Leopard print pants, a Beyoncé T-shirt and a pair of pink shorts are scattered around the audience, under the seats. A pink block with the bottom half of a mannequin, the bum facing towards the audience, is at one end of the stage. It is covered by pink, glittery, fabulous fabric. At the opposite end there is a larger pink block (there's enough room for two people to sit). Behind it, on the wall, is another pink glittery piece of fabric. It's a little bit tacky.

The stage is empty as the audience arrives. LUCY is operating the show from the tech box. Early era Beyoncé songs are playing ('Me Myself and I', 'Baby Boy' etc).

WILLY enters. The music cuts. He is wearing nothing but a pink towel, animal print socks and white trainers. He clutches the towel around his waist to cover himself. He is carrying a pink bucket of props in one hand, and his pink phone in the other. He has just got out of the shower and obviously late to do the show. He checks his phone intermittently.

He finds his leopard print pants and asks the audience to hold his towel up for him so he can put them on. Once they're on, he gives them his phone. He tells them that he is waiting for a text, and that they should let him know if it comes.

He waits.

He begins to make an anxiety gesture. He repeats it a few times, transforming it into a dance move.

He stops.

WILLY:

Lucy, there's meant to be music in the opening bit.

'Love on Top' by Beyoncé (an upbeat dance remix) plays loudly. He directs the anxiety dance move at the person with the phone, continuing to check if he's got a text. He hasn't. He gives up on that person. He finds his t-shirt under another chair and gets the audience to help him put it on. He gives them the phone, asking them to tell him if there's a text. He builds another anxiety gesture which turns into a dance move, adding it to the first move to establish a routine. The text doesn't come, he gives up on that person. He repeats this sequence of getting dressed/hold phone/dance move to put his shorts on. He now has a full routine.

The music abruptly cuts. He is interrupted by the Mannequin world. Here the music is not like Beyoncé at all. It is classical and foreboding. There is haze and blue lasers. It is ethereal and mythic. WILLY stares at the mannequin, taken off guard and slightly embarrassed.

This quickly disappears. The Beyoncé dance remix comes back and he continues his game with the audience. Faster, harder, more desperate for the text.

The phone dings, cutting the music. WILLY grabs it from the audience.

FUCK.

Oh, it's my mum.

I'm waiting for a text. Not from my mum.

Beat.

Lucy can you hold this and tell me if he texts please.

WILLY gives the phone to LUCY.

It's quite embarrassing actually because –

Last night was the first –

Beat.

Scene 2

Date.

WILLY is at the large block. This is the Date. It is bright and warm. There is a light underlying beat to this world, giving it drive, urgency and pace. This world is direct and performative.

I apologise.

'I'm sorry'

I say, 'It's never happened before.'

'It's never happened before.'

I excuse myself, and I go through the kitchen into the bathroom.

He makes his way to the bathroom which is stupid because it's such a small space.

I'm naked on this journey – which is risky, I know.

I lock the door.

Sound of door locking.

I turn on the tap.

Sound of tap being turned on and water running.

– so it sounds like I'm having a wee – and I look in the mirror at my floppy, flaccid, shrivelled…asleep…willy.

Beat.

Thank you for letting me down.

Thank you for making me look like an absolute mug.

And THANK YOU for being a wimp I mean it's a hole, it's a fucking hole.

Beat.

I stroke it gently to coax some life back into it. I splash some water on it to try and wake it up. I pull it a little bit, then I pull it down hard. I shake it. I pump it. I spit on it – and I want to fuck-ing smack it.

For a moment it looks like the spit is actually the kiss of life my willy needs, as it slowly rises to attention – like a happy turtle who is just waking up.

Yes. Good morning. About bloody time.

I turn off the tap.

Sound of tap being turned off.

I flush the toilet.

Sound of toilet flushing.

I go to run back into my room and say, 'Ooh I was just warming up…'

But it's a false alarm.

I flush the toilet again – *(toilet flush)* – which is probably a mistake as now because I've flushed twice he's gonna think I'm having a shit.

He jumps out of the Date, into one of the anxiety moves from the opening.

Any texts Lucy?

LUCY:

No

WILLY:

Fuck!

Scene 3

Backstory.

Hello, by the way. My name is Willy.

I'm twenty-seven years old and I am from Exeter.

I'm a massive Beyoncé fan. I have seen her six times, I'm on the tour DVD and she's touched my hand.

He lets an audience member touch his hand.

I also have a Beyoncé tattoo, in the form of a watermelon on my left ankle, just next to Simba.

WILLY shows his ankle.

This is in reference to her song 'Drunk in Love' where she sings 'I been drinking WATERMELON.' And I've only just recently realised that she doesn't actually mean she enjoys drinking the juice of this summer fruit, but rather watermelon is a metaphor for her husband Jay-Z's semen.

So I have a tattoo of Jay-Z's semen on my leg.

Typical Willy to get a tattoo of what I thought was a nice cute watermelon, when actually it's just cum.

Beat.

This is *Bottom*, the story of my quest for love.

And this –

He whips off the sheet covering the mannequin. It is wearing the same leopard print pants as WILLY. We faintly hear a short phrase of the Mannequin music.

– is my Bottom.

The Backstory music comes in. This is different to the Date and the Mannequin. It is electronic and synth-y.

The story begins when I moved this bottom to London. The Land of the Gays. I moved into an eight-bedroom warehouse flat with twenty people and a house rabbit in Hackney Wick…wanker…

I was bright-eyed, bushy-tailed, and tight-arsed.

WILLY checks in with himself.

Self-esteem?

He feels up the left mannequin leg.

Sky high.

Love for Beyoncé?

He feels up the right mannequin leg.

Endless.

Quest for love?

He squeezes the bum.

I've only just started – I'm gonna get out
there and find my man.

So I moved into the box room, and put all
my Beyoncé posters up to make myself
feel safe.

*WILLY crosses the stage and pulls down the
glittery sheet. It reveals loads of Beyoncé posters
stuck to the wall.*

Hello Bey.

BEYONCÉ:
Hello.

Scene 4

Date.

Doorbell.

He arrives late. Which is annoying.

I had timed it all perfectly. That means the fish has now been in the oven for over an hour, and that I've over-boiled the peas.

But I don't tell him this.

I pretend that it's fine and cover it by saying, 'Ooh I'm a shit cook, so please don't expect much.' (But actually it's not that I'm shit, it's that you're fucking late.)

I smile and sit down opposite him in my little kitchen, ignoring the smell of stale, dry fish. He picks up his fuck – *fork* – and asks me how I made it. I say, 'I've picked the fish from my garden, chopped the peas and I've shit in the pan.'

Yep, I've got no idea what I'm talking about. I can't even taste the food. It's gone all thick and furry. Like I'm chewing on a sock.

But he laughs. And his cheeks pinch in the corners which is cute, and I quickly forget that he was late.

Scene 5

WILLY dives out of the Date onto the floor and speaks whilst in a press-up position looking spannered at the ceiling. We snap into the Backstory.

I lost my virginity on Ketamin by the way, which is a horse tranquillizer. The guy asked me if I wanted to take some K and I said 'OK' – K… I don't remember it much at all.

I just remember seeing two different images of the ceiling as if my brain couldn't wire my eyes properly.

Scene 6

WILLY jumps back to the Date.

This is our third date – but I'm still fucking nervous – this is probably the most nervous I've ever been. It's up there with seeing Beyoncé in concert for the first time, and waiting for my mum to pick me up from the police station when I was caught stealing hair gel from Superdrug.

He is a Bottom. I can tell. It's like we have silently agreed that he is waiting for me to make the first move. I need to top his bottom, which is something I've never done before.

I am normally the gracious, welcoming, pillow-biting Bottom and I'm fucking nervous because all I keep thinking about trying to push into his wagon wheel and it's making me very sweaty.

Message ping. WILLY leaps out of Date with another anxiety move.

Lucy?

LUCY:
No

Scene 7

Present Day.

This third date happened last night. If it's 7:20 now, that was 23 hours, 20 mins ago.

I haven't slept a wink. My mate Bella says you always look you best when you haven't slept. She kept pulling all-nighters when she started going out with her boyfriend. Kind of like rough and ready. A bit stale...but fizzy. It worked for her, so...

I guesstimated when he would be home and texted him after one hour and twenty-five minutes. This way he will be able to give me full attention. No distractions.

I said –

WILLY gets the phone from LUCY.

I said, 'Thanks for last night.'

Maybe I should have asked him a question? Should I have put a kiss? There's nothing for him to respond to. 'Thanks for last night. Full stop.'

I know he's read because the double tick on WhatsApp has gone blue...so...

WILLY gives the phone back to LUCY.

Thanks Lucy.

Scene 8

Backstory.

I came to the Land of the Gays to find love,
which meant I had to 'go out' to look for
it. Which was expensive. So I found work
part-time. Part-time in four different jobs. I'm
a teaching assistant, a call centre operator, a
theatre usher, and – my main job – a waiter
in a burger restaurant.

*He grabs a pink mic and mic stand and works
the room. We hear the buzz of a restaurant.*

My job at the restaurant starts off quite fun.
I love looking after all the customers and
serving the drinks. Clearing the tables. They
don't put me on taking orders for the first

few weeks, but I don't mind as I quite like clearing the tables.

One of the managers has these plasticky cheeks and a nosey nose. She sits in her office every shift, and I have to bring up her staff meal which she orders around every two hours.

He sits down with the mic stand in the front row of the audience, facing the other side. This is the Restaurant. It is tight and claustrophobic.

When I first started, when I was bringing up her meal, she said:

'Ooh Willy – I was really happy when you interviewed for Belinda's Bangin' Burgerz. I love gay boys. I'm such a fag hag!'

She leant in closer to me. I could smell her.

'Ooh I bet you can't wait to get your hands on our meat!'

She smelled sweet and synthetic, like she'd rubbed a car air freshener under her armpits.

'So then, tell me Willy, are you a Top or a Bottom?'

Beat.

I said, 'Um…'

'Ah – obviously a Bottom then.' She winked and sank her brown teeth into a quarter pounder.

Scene 9

Mannequin.

WILLY considers himself.

Am I a Top or a Bottom?

He inspects the mannequin.

He can't decide.

He starts to pull down the pants, to look at the bottom –

WILLY:

No.

He pulls up the pants with a snap.

Scene 10

Backstory. WILLY sits on the edge of the manne-quin block.

I get home after that shift and I open my laptop.

Google Chrome

Gaytube

Blowjobs

Anal

Bareback

WILLY checks in.

Self-esteem?

Great.

Love for Beyoncé?

Also great.

Quest for Love?

Currently unsuccessful.

Maybe I should stop wanking and get
on Tinder.

Scene 11

WILLY goes to his bucket of props and pulls out a pink ukulele.

…and it's not a fringe show unless you've learnt three chords on the ukulele…

WILLY goes and sits in the audience.

Top or Bottom?

I went on Tinder and I matched with Brian

He looked quite hunky with a Hawaiian – shirt

I thought he looked really handsome

He said 'Hello Willy how you are you?'

I said 'I'm fine thanks, what are you up to tonight? To-night?'

He said 'Top or Bottom?'

TOP or BOTTOM?

TOP or BOTTOM?

I went on Tinder and I matched with John-o

He looked handsome with a mono-brow

Which I thought I could handle

He said 'Hello Willy you look saucy'

I said 'Hello John-o ooh I do quite like

condiments…what's your favourite?'

He took a second to respond

He said 'Top or Bottom?'

TOP or BOTTOM?

TOP or BOTTOM?

Text message ping.

…Lucy who is that please?

LUCY:

Er it's your flatmate, he says that the kitch–

WILLY:

OK – don't worry – it's fine.

WILLY continues to sing.

I went on Tinder matched with Susan –
But she wasn't my type
But she's here tonight…say hello Susan

WILLY picks someone in the audience to be Susan. Gets them to wave.

Hello Susan!

I went on Tinder and I matched with Alec
He had a nice smile and a phallic – cactus
in his profile picture
I said 'Hello Alec how's your cactus?'
He said 'Hello Willy do you like my prick?'
I said 'Yeah it looks lovely…'
He said 'Top or Bottom?'

TOP or BOTTOM?
TOP or BOTTOM?

Before you make friction

You gotta make a decision

Before you make friction

What's your position?

Top? Or Bottom?

Scene 12

Sex Facts.

WILLY strides up and down the stage, like a know-it-all professor giving a lecture.

In general we can say there are two categories for bum sex.

WILLY goes to his bucket and gets out a pink top hat and a pink beret.

Top –

He puts the top hat on someone.

– and Bottom.

He puts the beret on someone on the opposite side.

In sex the Top is the penetrator and the Bottom is the penetrated. The fucker and the fucked.

Now I am not an expert, but I think biology gives heterosexual relationships a clue as to who is going to be the Top and who is going to be the Bottom. BUT with Queer relationships that kind of goes out the window. But we still try and stick to these binary rules…because Humans like rules.

Nowadays people are clear on their Tinder or Grindr profiles what they are looking for, by either stating it in their 'about me' section, or asking 'Top or Bottom?' very early on in the conversation. So that you can match with the right position.

And to identify with this can be as normal as saying…'I am wearing tiger print socks.'

WILLY chooses a few audience members and says an obvious fact about them. 'I am wearing a fabulous knitted jumper' etc.

So – once we define our position, the rules are set, and we can play the game of sex.

Thanks, Lucy.

LUCY plays 'You Sexy Thing (I Believe In Miracles)' by Hot Chocolate. WILLY dances as if doing a Soul Train. He is shit at it.

In the 70s, queer men who didn't have the internet and had to meet people in real life used hankies as a down-low code to indicate their sexual preference.

WILLY pulls out a purple hanky and a leopard print hanky from his pockets.

If you put the hanky out your left back pocket you were a Top, and out the right you were a Bottom. And different colours suggested that you were into different things – if you had a purple hanky you liked piercings –

He gives the purple hanky to someone.

– or leopard print if you liked tattoos –

He gives the leopard print hanky to someone.

He pulls out a yellow hanky.

– or yellow if you liked piss.

Susan.

He gives the yellow hanky to Susan.

Thanks Lucy.

Music stops.

But there is a problem – what happens if I fancy someone who is the same position as me? How do I get past that? Have I missed the love of my life because we've both put down the same thing?

WILLY moves to the Date.

Before I met this guy I'd been a Bottom. I didn't know what it felt like to be a Top because I'd never even tried it. And I didn't know if you could change yourself once you've labelled yourself.

Scene 13

Date.

He looks at me straight in the eyes when we speak which is kind of freaky so I keep playing with the peas on my plate with my fork. Mashing them up to make mushy peas.

I'm gripping my fork quite tightly and it slips out my hand and lands on the floor behind me. I bend down to pick it up, but I realise I'm showing him my bum – I don't want to give him the wrong impression so I turn around quickly to show him my crotch.

I wonder what he's thinking.

Probably how amazing the sex is going to be when I finally top him.

Or, 'what the fuck is this guy doing he is obviously a Bottom I need to leave.' Please don't leave.

I worry that he might think I am a Bottom because of what I'm wearing. Or because of how I sound. Or because I'm not very strong.

I try and give off the 'Top vibe.' Controlled, strong and heavy. I plant my legs and puff out

my chest. I square out my shoulders and I
put a smile on my face which says, 'Hey –
I'm a Top.'

Mannequin music plonks in. WILLY is distracted.

He puts up his hand to stop it.

Shut up.

Back to Date.

I'm a Top.

Scene 14

Backstory.

*WILLY starts to melt out of the scene and into
the crowd bottom-first. 'Dreamer' by Livin' Joy
supports it. He goes through the centre row of the
audience as moving through a busy club.*

I was at Uni in Manchester when I came out
– when I say 'came out' I mean drunkenly
fell into some guy's face in a club in front of
my friends. I started this weird non-sexual
relationship with a guy. He took me by the
hand and dragged me around Canal Street –
the 'gay village' – showing me the clubs, pubs
and bars and telling me about gay culture.

He pointed at the muscley 'straight-acting'
guys and said they were the Tops, and pointed
at the camp, skinny, flamboyant twinks and
said they were the Bottoms.

I doubted that was true and wondered how
he knew that. Like how would you know?

But I was naïve. This was my first dipping
into 'queer culture.' And I soon learnt that
this part of queer culture was the loudest,
whitest, and the G-A-Y-est.

WILLY picks up the phone from LUCY and checks it. No messages. He gives it back, picks up the ukulele and heads to the other side of the audience.

Do You Like Wearing Pink

Do you like wearing make-up and do you like wearing pink?
You're a Bottom!

Do you like going to the pub and having a pint?
You're a Top!

WILLY asks the audience.

Do you like *Sex And The City* and Angel Delight?

If the answer is yes, then:

You're a Bottom!

WILLY makes some questions up on the spot. It is silly and has nothing to do with anything. 'Do

you like going swimming in the middle of winter
with carrots up your nose' etc. He quizzes them,
judging them, moves through them and shouts
over to the other side.

Do you prefer Beyoncé or Rihanna?

He keeps asking until someone says Beyoncé.

What's your favourite Beyoncé song?

He isn't happy with their answer. He asks around
until he hears a song he likes. He teases people. He
calls his favourite suggestion a Top, and everyone
else who suggested a song a Bottom.

WILLY stands in front of his posters and looks
to Beyoncé.

Beyoncé.
I like you, but I also like pints.
I've never seen *Sex And The City*, but I love
the colour pink.
Am I a Top or a Bottom?

BEYONCÉ:

I think a star is born a star. I think…I know
me…I was born to do what I do. It's just too
natural. There's certain things that I know
no one taught me. No one can teach you. It's
just…you are.

Scene 15

Date.

I clear the plates and ask if he wants a taste of
my dessert.

Our dessert.

THE dessert.

The fucking spotted dick I bought from
Sainsbury's yesterday because it was reduced.
50p for two dicks.

He says yes.

I guess I had this idea that he would say yes to the spotted dick, and that would be the signal to rip each other's clothes off and roll around the kitchen floor.

But this doesn't happen.

Instead I do a nervous laugh –

'Hahaha'

– and accidentally inhale as the spoon goes into my mouth. Some of it goes down the wrong hole and I make a stupid joke –

'Ooh I'm choking on spotted dick.'

Why the fuck did I say that. Why the fuck have I given him spotted dick – does this mean he'll think I've got syphilis? I wonder if I should tell him that I'm clean and that I've recently been tested…

We finish the dick and he offers to do the washing up.

'Yes actually that would be quite nice as I am tired and very nervous and that was a big effort.'

But I say no

'No'

and leave it for the morning.

Scene 16

Sex Facts.

Generic shopping channel music/lift music plays. It has a samba beat. WILLY is the know-it-all professor again. He step-ball-changes throughout.

When bottoming there are a few things I do to prepare my body.

Unless I want to shit everywhere, I use
a douche.

*WILLY goes into the bucket and pulls out a pink
douche and jar of chocolate spread.*

You fill this up with water, you stick it up
your bum, and it washes the shit away. Not
everybody uses this. Not everybody wants to,
not everybody needs to and not everybody
has to. And some people just hope for the
best. Don't they Susan.

*WILLY nods at Susan and puts the douche down
next to the mannequin.*

I also watch what I eat. No curries or
anything spicy. You don't want any nasty
surprises.

*There is a rhythmic pause in the music. WILLY
has been trying to time the speech to so that it
lands with the next line.*

You have to time it right.

So, if you want to douche and do all that, you have to pre-arrange. Or at least prepare for the possibility.

Thanks Lucy.

Music cuts.

They don't show this bit in porn. In real life you can't ever be spontaneous. It isn't attractive.

'Oh…hi yeah…sexy time – hang on let me go clean the shit out of my arse.'

It doesn't work.

Backstory creeps in. No longer know-it-all professor.

It's quite stressful. You have to plan really far ahead for a one night stand with a stranger you haven't even met yet.

This all started to get difficult to manage. So I started getting fucking smashed so I didn't have to worry about it.

Scene 17

Mannequin.

WILLY pretends to be a Dom Top in a club.

The jar of chocolate spread becomes a drink. He aggressively objectifies the mannequin, leering at it, touching it etc.

He pulls down the mannequin's pants, spits on it, then smears chocolate spread on the bum and legs.

He continues being the Dom Top until he sits down at the mic and snaps to –

Scene 18

Restaurant.

He licks the chocolate off his fingers, as if finishing a burger.

'Ooh Willy! I've just had a quick meeting with Big Boss Belinda – don't worry you're not in any trouble! We are both really happy with how you're getting on at Belinda's Bangin' Burgerz, and – now we don't normally do this – but we'd like to offer you an early promotion to…drum roll please… Table Service Waiter! Yaaas Kween! – *(He snaps his fingers like in Rupaul's Drag Race.)* – So here is your bum bag (oooh!), here is your float, and here is your pen and pad. But be careful. Because if you lose any money, or if the card receipts don't balance, you're going to have to pay for it yourself. It's a big responsibility. OK hun, off you go! Byeeeee!' *(Snaps fingers.)*

Scene 19

Backstory.

Working the four jobs can be difficult to
juggle. I begin to lose sleep worrying about
paying rent. My room gets messy and my
washing piles up.

But when I moved to London I made friends
really quickly. I got in with a 'cool' gang that
I knew through a friend. We go out every
Friday and Saturday. We get drunk and
smashed up. I'm the only queer person in
the group so all the girls love me and all the
boys are intrigued. They're older than me by a
couple of years so it always feels like I'm being
looked after.

They threw me a watermelon party for my
twenty-fifth birthday with watermelon

bunting, watermelon hat, watermelon
sunglasses, and a watermelon.

*WILLY walks to the bucket of props and pulls
out the items he describes. He puts them on,
wrapping himself in the bunting.*

At this point I think the reference to Beyoncé
is getting lost, because if they really knew me
they'd know that I like watermelon because
I liked Beyoncé and they would throw me a
fucking Beyoncé party. Instead I'm just Willy
the Watermelon Boy. And I'm still no closer
to finding love.

We went out to a club.

*Club music starts playing, we hear snippets
of Beyoncé singing 'Love On Top'. WILLY is
clutching the watermelon, looking lost.*

We were smashed and pretty fucked up. I had
lost the gang so was on my own. It was the

end of the night and I was desperate to go home with someone, so I could tell everyone the next day on the group WhatsApp. It was also quite far away from where I lived and I didn't want to go all the way home.

This guy was all in white, like an angel. I was so smashed that I didn't even know what he looked like until we were in the back of the taxi. We ended up in Balham, which was even further away from where I lived. He took me inside and gave me some orange juice. I offered him some of my drugs but he said he was 'completely sober' and he 'didn't touch that stuff.' Which is a bit weird.

We went into his bedroom. He asked me about the watermelons and said, 'Yeah of course you like Beyoncé, could you be any gay-er.'

WILLY takes off the sunglasses, embarrassed.

We showered together, and he asked me if he could piss on me. I said 'OK.' He topped me. Twice. I couldn't get an erection, so I couldn't top him even if I wanted to.

He pours water from the douche onto the mannequin.

I get home, de-watermelon and open my laptop:

He takes off the watermelon items and sits on the edge of the mannequin block.

Google Chrome

Gaytube

Blowjobs

Anal

Bareback

WILLY tries to check in.

Self-esteem?

GREAT! Sure.

Love for Beyoncé?

Don't even look at me Bey.

Quest for Love?

I'm not sure how long I can keep this up.
Need to work out if I'm a Top or a Bottom.

Walk of shame quietly across the space to the Date. Before he gets there –

I go on Google.

TOPS:
What's it like having your dick in someone's ass? What does it feel like?
… Umm nice and warm and wet, kind of like

warm apple pie.

It's just nice. It's like 'thank you'.

…this is great, this is everything I need and
more. 'Thank you.'

Scene 20

Date.

We go into my bedroom.

This is quite forward of me but it feels like a
natural progression. I don't have a living room
and the kitchen still smells of overcooked
stale fish.

My room is so small the only thing you can
do is sit on my bed.

Beat.

I look at my room as if for the first time to
try and work out what he might be thinking.

The four walls are covered floor to ceiling

in Beyoncé posters and magazine cutouts.

And I feel silly. Silly Willy the Pissed-On

Watermelon Boy.

I wonder if I should take some of them down.

We lie on my bed.

I'm deliberately not touching him, as if the

touch of my hand will magically dissolve our

clothes and leave me whimpering with my

willy out. I end up kind of awkwardly curving

my body around him, leaving about two

inches of space between us.

Scene 21

*Backstory. The worlds are merging. Backstory
music plays, we faintly hear Beyoncé singing
'Love On Top' over it. It's dark and bassy.*

The last time I had sex before this was with a Tinder match called Duncan. In his picture he's got these shades on and his face slightly turned away from the camera. I like his air of mystery.

Duncan comes over. He's really tall and has a massive spot on his nose that you can't stop looking at. He doesn't look much like his picture, but I couldn't see much of his face in it anyway. We have two bottles of wine and I watch him get slowly drunk.

Then I bring out my MKAT and we snort it off the kitchen table.

An hour later and I'm rubbing his back as he's being sick in my freshly planted pansies on our little roof terrace. The sick lands on my socks and splashes up my arms – but I don't mind, we've all been drunk. I lend him my toothbrush to clean himself up with, as any honourable gentleman would do.

He stumbles into my bedroom and rips off his clothes. He asks me to turn around so he can fuck me.

I said 'OK.'

I give him a condom to use, but he moans and says that it's too tight. And he takes it off halfway through without telling me.

I didn't see him again.

WILLY gets to the mannequin and pulls off the pants. He goes down to the floor and tears both legs off. He struggles with it, it takes time.

Has he text me, Lucy?

LUCY:
No, sorry Willy.

WILLY:

Silly Willy. (You need to protect yourself.)

WILLY picks up the bum of the mannequin and cradles it. He carries it throughout the next scene.

Can you put some Beyoncé on please?

LUCY plays 'Love On Top'. It is mixed with the bass line of the Backstory music so it feels slightly distorted. WILLY must speak louder to be heard.

Scene 22

I take on extra hours at the restaurant as people are off sick –

TOPS:

What is it like having your dick in some-one's ass?

WILLY ignores it.

WILLY:

I start cutting out lunch because I don't
have time to eat properly between jobs – but
it's OK because I can eat leftovers at work.
Someone says I look 'quite thin'…which I
take as a compliment.

My manager sits me down at the end of a
busy shift. We only had two waiters when
there is normally four. We ran out of burgers
halfway through and I had to go to Tesco's to
get some backup.

I squeeze into her office, I'm basically sat on
her lap.

*WILLY leans into the Restaurant world, speaking
into the microphone.*

'Ooh Willy I've just counted up your card
receipts and your money doesn't balance.
You're £90 short.'

She throws a card receipt at me.

It says '£90. DECLINED'

Which means a card payment had declined
but I cashed it off as if I'd accepted it.

'You need to give me £90 hun. That comes
out of your pocket babe. You are £90 short.'

£90?

*WILLY frantically starts to collect the rest of
the mannequin, protecting himself, trying and
failing to put it back together.*

£90 is about a day's work. Or a month's
food shop.

We had two waiters instead of four and it's my
fault I make a mistake? But it's a casual job,
and if I don't pay this then I won't have a job.

WILLY climbs onto the mannequin block, clutching all the mannequin parts. The chocolate spread has begun to rub off onto his clothes.

I want to tell her that it's bullshit and spit in her plasticky face.

I get tense. Hot and fire like I'm this massive fireball of sweat and flames that will burn this cunt to a crisp.

'Love On Top' is interrupted by –

TOPS:

WHAT IS IT LIKE HAVING YOUR D–

WILLY:

Lucy where's Beyoncé gone?

'Love On Top' comes back as the song hits the first key change. WILLY steps down from the box and quickly but carefully puts the legs on

*the floor. He is still holding the bum. He goes to
face the manager.*

No – listen – listen – I have moved to this
city to find –

*The music is too loud. She can't hear him. He
grabs the microphone.*

Listen. I have moved to this city to find
friends and to find love. But I spend all my
time here, with you, or at my other jobs, so
between that I'm just swiping on this fucking
APP trying to find someone to have this
love with – *(He turns to LUCY doing the first
anxious dance move.)* – Lucy has he text me?
*(WILLY turns back to the manager, continuing
the anxious dance routine throughout this
speech. It grows and gets chaotic.)* And I am
tired – I go out all weekend and I spend all
my money getting fucked on drugs and dick,
trying to FEEL something with people –

that I know when I'm sober, I won't FEEL anything for. So by Sunday, I'm still tired, I'm on comedown but now I'm BROKE. *(He gets stuck in one move, spinning on the spot.)* So by Sunday, I'm still tired, I'm on comedown but now I'm BROKE. So by Sunday, I'm still tired, I'm on comedown but now I'm BROKE. *(WILLY dashes to the mannequin legs.)* Self-esteem – love for Beyoncé – quest for love. *(He launches back to the manager, desperately pushing the dance.)* So I take on extra shifts, spending even more time with you, here at Belinda's Fucking Burgerz trying to pay my rent, buy my food shop and just fucking EXIST in this shit storm of living a hundred miles an hour. *(The song has ended. He stops dancing.)* So fuck you. Fuck your £90. AND FUCK YOUR BURGERS.

Pause.

But I say 'OK'.

I go to the cash machine and I punch in my numbers.

I smile as I give her the cash. Because I'm a fucking twat.

I get home and open my laptop:

As he speaks, WILLY slowly collects the rest of the mannequin. He carries it with him to the Date.

Google Chrome

Gaytube

Blowjobs

Anal

Bareback

Google Chrome

Gaytube

Blowjobs

Anal

Bareback

Google Chrome

Gaytube

Blowjobs

Anal

Bareback

Google Chrome

Gaytube

Blowjobs

Anal

Bareback

Google Chrome

Gaytube

Blowjobs

Anal

Bareback

Google Chrome

Gaytube

Blowjobs

Anal

Bareback

WILLY sits in the Date.

Kiss me please, I just want to be something.

Lucy do I have a text?

The Date music is back but it is not complete. It is missing beats, struggling to continue.

We talk about TV, films and music. He looks at my Beyoncé limited edition DVD and CD collection and I'm gonna top the fuck out of you. He says he's a 'big fan' of Bey and his favourite song is 'Schoolin' Life' – and I'm like how does this work? Where do I put my body? How do I move it? What if I'm shit? What if I'm so completely shit that he pulls off, walks off, and blocks me on Tinder? – 'Schoolin' Life'? – I can see Beyoncé staring down on my giving me her Sasha Fierce eye, she's got this look which says, 'Yeah go on mate' – 'Schoolin' Life' –

Beat.

Nobody says 'Schoolin' Life'.

That's my favourite song.

WILLY gently puts all the mannequin parts down.

Without breaking his gaze I take a deep
breath and put my hand on his leg.

He puts his hand on top of mine.

I breathe in and I breathe out – and I wonder
if I should get my inhaler.

I'm close enough to smell his sweat and it's
mixed with the overcooked fish that has
wafted in from the kitchen.

He looks amazing…but I don't tell him this.

I take one last look at Beyoncé. She nods.

We both lean in, until our mouths touch.

I close my eyes,

and I really hope this is OK.

Beat.

A faint chime from the Mannequin music is heard. It is delicate and bare.

WILLY collects the mannequin.

I apologise.

'I'm sorry.'

I say 'it's never happened before.'

'It's never happened before.'

He walks across the stage as he speaks. He is covered in chocolate spread, carrying the mannequin, carrying himself.

I excuse myself, and I go through the kitchen into the bathroom.

I'm naked on this journey – which is risky, I know.

I lock the door.

He places the mannequin on the floor.

I turn on the tap – so it sounds like I'm
having a wee – and I look in the mirror at my
floppy, flaccid, shrivelled…asleep…willy.

I think about every time I've had sex.
I think about drugs.
I think about relationships.
I think about porn
I think about erections
I think about my jobs
I think about how all I want is to speak to
someone properly, about what I'm really
thinking.

How I want the spark in my chest to burst
into tiny stars that shoot out of my eyes and
into his heart so that he knows I am worth
something and I'm not just a Bottom.

I'm not just a Bottom.

WILLY puts his mannequin back together on the block. He is careful. Looking after himself.

The mannequin is complete. The music stops.

I'm not just a Bottom.

You're not just a Bottom.

Pause.

I open the door and head back to my bedroom.

WILLY steps towards the Date.

He's still here, looking at my Beyoncé magazine collection – which isn't really for touching.

And I say:

'OK.

I think I have a problem with getting an erection.

And this is the first time I've tried to have sex when I haven't been smashed so it's quite new.

And it's the first time I've tried to top somebody. So please bear with me.'

Beat.

But he says 'It's OK.'

He doesn't actually mind if he tops or he bottoms.

And that if it's OK with me he would still like to stay and just watch TV.

Beat

Which is nice.

So I open my laptop.

WILLY crosses to sit in the Date.

Google Chrome

Netflix

Orange is the New Black

I've already seen this episode, but I don't
mind watching it twice.

After about ten minutes I put my arm around
him *(WILLY puts his arm around the space next
to him, around the guy)* and he puts his head
on my shoulder – and for a moment I feel
like he's trying to have sex again…!

But I look down to see that his eyes are
closed.

But he's not dead. He's asleep. The muscles
on his face have all relaxed, like they do when

you're asleep, so he looks a bit creased. But he still looks really good.

Orange is the New Black finishes and Netflix does that thing where it automatically plays the next episode. I want to sleep myself, so I reach out to shut the lid of my laptop, but I can't reach it without disturbing him.

> *WILLY tries to reach the laptop with his legs, but can't move as his arm is still around the guy.*

I don't want to wake him and cause him any more hassle so I just leave it there playing.

The weight of his body leaning on mine feels nice. I feel like I'm looking after him or something. Like he should feel safe with me.

> *WILLY carefully edges his arm out from behind the guy, so as not to disturb him. He reaches behind the block to pick up the ukulele.*

Top or Bottom (You Didn't Ask Me)

You messaged me on Tinder

I thought you had kind eyes

You messaged me quite quickly

And it took me by surprise

You asked me what I was up to

I said I was drinking tea

I waited for the question...

But you didn't ask me

You didn't ask me

Top or Bottom?

You didn't ask me

Top or Bottom?

You didn't ask me

Top, or Bottom

If you don't mind holding on

I think I'd rather just sit

get to know you a bit instead

Of this complicated shit

Tell me where you're from?

What's your story?

What makes you laugh?

What do you want to be?

Cos you didn't ask me

Top or Bottom?

You didn't ask me

Top or Bottom?

You didn't ask me

Top, or Bottom

Will you fill me with fire

All the bubbly feelings

Will you be patient

cos I might need healing

I can give you warm hugs

And I can kind of cook

We could stay up talking

Or maybe read a book

There's a million things to find out

Before we go to bed

A million things to find out

Before you ask me –

There's a million things to find out

Before we go to bed

A million things to find out

Before you ask me –

There's a million things to find out

Before we go to bed

A million things to find out

Before you ask me –

Top or Bottom?

Top or Bottom?

Cus you didn't ask me

Phones dings.

Please tell me that's him.

LUCY:

Yeah it is.

Blackout.

WWW.OBERONBOOKS.COM

Follow us on Twitter @oberonbooks
& Facebook @OberonBooksLondon

Printed in the USA
CPSIA information can be obtained
at www.ICGtesting.com
LVHW020958171024
794056LV00004B/1211

9 781786 827388